*Healthcare is a skyrocketing $6 Trillion Global Opportunity*

# Healthcare

*Will U.S. Politics Kill Our Opportunity?*

EDMUND L. VALENTINE

ISBN: 0984047875
ISBN-13: 978-0-9840478-7-1

# DEDICATION

This book is dedicated to the people of the United States who encompass all that is great and all that is wanting in a society ruled by a democracy. We are at a pivotal point in our history...one road will reinvigorate our great country, the other will destine us to become a second-tier power. A critical turning point is how we capitalize on the global healthcare opportunity.

# CONTENTS

# ACKNOWLEDGMENTS

This book would never have been possible without the extensive work conducted by MMC International in its ongoing annual fact-based reviews of the trends shaping the healthcare industry. It would never have been written without the discussion with a number of friends whose strong political views challenged, encouraged, and shocked me into writing this book.

# 1 INTRODUCTION

I love the United States with all my heart. I still get goose bumps when I hear the Star Spangled Banner and God Bless America. To me, it is an honor and a privilege to say the Pledge of Allegiance...and as frustrated and sometimes as mad as I get, I am unbelievably proud of the fact that people in the United States can say what they think and openly argue their views without fear of government reprisal...no matter how stupid they may, at times, seem to me.

My seven and a half years in the military taught me that if you give people a chance, they will rise to the occasion. I have seen valor in combat situations from the least likely people...and seen unexpected generosity and compassion. What I learned was that if you give people a chance and provide them with objective facts, they have enough common sense to come to the right conclusion and to do the right things.

To me, the role of government is to do those things that individuals or companies would not or could not do on their own but which are needed for the benefit of the majority of the population. Furthermore, how a country takes care of its disadvantaged shows its values.

Besides the United States Constitution, three things have enabled our great nation: 1) education, 2) industrialization, and 3) "constructive greed"…which I define as the ability to accumulate and retain significant personal wealth through the development of economic drivers, e.g., technologies, products and/or companies, that create jobs and which benefit United States economic growth.

Not much gets done by people that are happy and content. We are only driven to do something by two emotions: 1) fear that something is going to happen if we do not act, or 2) the ability to benefit if we take some action. So, financial and tax incentives have to be in place to entice individuals to make the personal commitment and to take the personal and/or financial risks required to create economic drivers. People will not take risks without a sufficiently large related reward. China has studied the United States and understands this and has been putting this entrepreneurial system in place.

Industrialization results from a combination of technology, systems, processes, legislation and/or regulation, standards, markets and customers. All have to come together to allow for industrialization...and today they are coming together in healthcare. Industrialization means standardization, a continual pursuit of quality and cost reduction, and competition-driven price decreases until the product and/or service becomes a relatively low-priced commodity.

This is opportune because today: 1) we are the world leaders in pharmaceuticals, medical devices, in vitro diagnostics, medical equipment, and medical supplies, and 2) five base technologies are coming together to revitalize these industries. Whether we retain <u>high technology</u> medical product innovation and manufacturing in this country is fully dependent upon the financial incentives and tax policies which apply to these industries. The wrong policies will continue to drive these high-paying, high-technology jobs overseas.

U.S. healthcare is a $2.8 trillion industry that employs in excess of 17 million Americans. Our fragmented healthcare enterprise, which delivers the best healthcare in the world, is unbelievably inefficient. It wastes in excess of one trillion dollars annually, almost seven percent of our 2012 $15 trillion gross domestic product.(GDP). It is ripe for industrialization which will yield new products, systems and processes that will have global markets.

However, for the first time in my life, I am deeply concerned. Our country and political system, in my opinion, are being destroyed by vested interests, special interest groups, and misinformation. If our country does not address four issues (healthcare, education, taxation, and immigration), we will continue on a path to becoming a second-tier economy…and our middle class and standard of living will become a distant memory. This is the reason I wrote this book, "Healthcare", and "Multi-Trillion Dollar U.S. HEALTHCARE TO 2020 Gold Rush".

# 2 HEALTHCARE IS DESTROYING THE MIDDLE CLASS

The increasing cost of healthcare, if not corrected, will compromise our ability to compete on a global basis. We spend from five percent to ten percent more of our gross domestic product (GDP) on healthcare (HC) than any major developed country[1] (countries that have universal healthcare coverage) or developing country. If uncorrected, healthcare costs will compromise our global cost competitiveness as healthcare is a cost component in every product we produce.

---

[1] Comparison is based on the thirty-three Organization for Economic Cooperation and Development (OECD) countries.

Rising healthcare costs, if not contained, will destroy the "American Dream" and our middle class. According to a Rand study, between 1999 and 2009, the median-income for the typical American family of four grew by about $22,920, from $76,200 in 1999 to $99,120 in 2009 (in 2009 constant dollars). Increases in the prices of consumer goods and non-healthcare taxes absorbed fifty-two percent of the increase. Most of the rest was consumed by higher healthcare co-pays, deductibles, drug and medical supplies costs. This left our average American family with only $1,140 more disposable income per year in 2009 versus 1999, $95 more per month. If taxes had kept pace with the growth in federal healthcare spending for Medicare, Medicaid and other public health programs, instead of deficit financing, during the same period, our typical American family would have paid an additional $4,680 in taxes in 2009. This would have reduced average family disposable income by $3,540 in 2009 versus 1999 – significantly decreasing personal disposable income and our overall quality of life[2].

---

[2] Note: No single data source can provide a complete picture of an average family's finances. The Rand study utilized reasonable assumptions in preparing their income estimates. Net health insurance benefits were factored in net of tax benefits. Annual incomes include employer-paid health insurance premium contributions as they more accurately represent changes in healthcare costs and contributions over time.

Historically, the cost of care has been obscured for most of us. However, employees are facing increases in cost-sharing and out-of-pocket expenses which is making more of us increasingly sensitive to the true cost of healthcare. The steep decline in access and affordability of healthcare, if not corrected, will destroy the "American Dream" and our middle class.

---

Sources: Auerbach DI and Kellermann AL, "A Decade of Healthcare Cost Growth Has Wiped Out Real Income Gains for an Average U.S. Family," Health Affairs, Vol. 30, No. 9, September 2011. David I. Auerbach is a health economist at RAND in Boston, Massachusetts and Arthur L. Kellermann is vice president and director of RAND Health, in Santa Monica, California.

EDMUND L. VALENTINE

# 3 WE CAN FIX U.S. HEALTHCARE

We have to undertake five initiatives to fix our healthcare system:

1. Convert our paper medical records and information to electronic medical records and information;
2. Migrate provider compensation from procedures to outcomes and from fee-for-service to wellness;
3. Transform health insurance into a commodity product;
4. Enable the industrialization of U.S. healthcare; and
5. Insure the financial incentives and tax policies are in place to retain high technology medical products, systems, and processes innovation and product manufacturing in the United States.

These initiatives are being enabled by the convergence of five base technologies that are allowing the innovation of additional combination technologies and new products, systems and processes to streamline healthcare, improve quality, increase patient satisfaction, and decrease costs.

1. Computer hardware
2. Software
3. Wi-Fi
4. Internet
5. Genomics

However, vested interests, special interest groups, and misinformation are challenging our ability to implement healthcare reform. Healthcare is a global opportunity that can revitalize our economy while improving care, increasing lifespans, decreasing suffering and deaths, and lowering our healthcare costs.

# 4 GLOBAL
## HEALTHCARE OPPORTUNITY

Global healthcare is a skyrocketing ~$6.5 trillion industry that is positioned for explosive growth[3]. The world population is forecast to increase by 1.3 billion between now and 2030, from seven billion in 2012 to 8.3 billion in 2030[4]. During the same period, the global middle class is forecast to grow an unprecedented 2.5 times, from about 2.0 billion today to around five billion in 2030[5]. Simultaneously, the

---

[3] Based upon IMF estimate of GDP by country for 2010 multiplied by World Health Organization's World Health Statistics 2008 healthcare expenditures as a percent of GDP.

[4] U.S. Census Bureau – World POPClock Projection and United Nations World Population Prospects.

[5] McKinsey and Co. middle class estimated growth and MMC International analysis.

≥65 population with their increasing lifespans and growing number of chronic conditions is forecast to grow by 436 million people - almost doubling to 998 million[6]. In addition, the urban population is forecast to grow by 1.5 billion from 2012 to 2030, providing increased access to healthcare facilities and services.

The aging global population will: 1) have increasing access to healthcare, 2) demand western medicine treatments and related products, and 3) have an exploding ability to pay for western medical products and treatments. In addition, health spending will continue to rise faster than the gross domestic product (GDP) in virtually all countries - magnifying gaps in budget deficits and spurring governments to invest in products and technologies that will decrease healthcare costs.

Simultaneously, enabling computer hardware, software, materials, wi-fi, internet, genomics, organ transplant, and manufacturing technologies and innovations are converging to begin the industrialization of healthcare. Industrialization means standardization, automation, implementation of cost-

---

[6] United States Census Bureau International Programs, 2012.

effective technologies and systems, consistent quality improvements, decreasing costs, and lower prices.

Industrialization created the United States economy, our middle class, and raised our standard of living. The magnitude of the emerging global healthcare opportunity has the potential to invigorate economic growth, create high-technology, high-paying jobs, and improve our standard of living.

The majority of pharmaceuticals, high-volume diagnostics, medical devices, medical equipment, and medical supplies are now commodities. Most commodity products can be locally manufactured or outsourced for manufacturing to the lowest-cost, quality manufacturing countries. The opportunity for the United States resides in exploiting emerging technologies to innovate, develop and market new, unique products designed to reduce overall healthcare costs while improving treatment outcomes and/or patient wellness and/or quality of life.

The opportunity has not been missed by either developed or the major emerging economies, e.g., China, India, Russia and Brazil. As an example, China's central and provincial governments have targeted and are making significant investments in health-related research, innovation, development, manufacturing, and delivery.

The United States is in the best position to capitalize on this opportunity. It is the leader in the innovation, development and global commercialization of pharmaceuticals and high technology medical devices, in vitro diagnostics, medical equipment and medical supplies. It is well positioned to be the leader in cybernetics, personalized medicine, wellness, and interoperable healthcare systems/software.

Today, the United States, which represents about 43% of the global healthcare market, is the largest healthcare market in the world. We, the United States population, have a preference for the latest high technology products/solutions. Our fragmented healthcare industry wastes in excess of $1 trillion annually, more than 40 percent of healthcare expenditures.

The United States healthcare industry negatives can be changed into an opportunity upon which we can capitalize to reinvigorate our economy and to put it on a more sustainable growth trajectory. The $1 trillion in healthcare waste is starting to be and can be utilized to create cost-sharing incentives to develop products/offerings that will extract costs while improving outcomes, patient wellness and/or quality of life. Many of the innovations will find global markets.

To put the ≥$1 trillion available annually, for the foreseeable future, in perspective, we don't need to look any further than historic United State technology investments. Between 1940 and 2010, we invested a combined total of $543.9 billion, in 2012 dollars, in the three largest United States federally funded scientific programs. Each program has yielded significant economic, employment and quality of life benefits for all Americans.

- The Manhattan Project (1940 to 1945, cost $31 billion[7], an average $6.2 billion annually, in 2012 dollars) enabled the use of atomic energy

---

[7] Sources: Richard G. Hewlett and Oscar E. Anderson, Jr., The New World: A History of the United States Atomic Energy Commission, Volume 1, 1939/1946 (Oak Ridge, Tennessee: U.S. AEC Technical Information Center, 1972), pp. 723-724. Includes capital and operations costs from 1942 through 1945. Costs adjusted using a base year of 1944 (the year of highest Manhattan Project expenditures). Actual costs per facility per year are apparently unknown. Bureau of Labor Statistics CPI Inflation Calculator to convert into 2012 dollars.

(e.g., power plants, radioactivity, the atom bomb, etc.).

- Space Flight (1959 to 2015, cost $507 billion[8], an average $8.9 billion annually, in 2012 dollars) yielded advances in robotics, materials, computers, software, and communications (e.g., communication satellites). It resulted in the creation of thousands of companies that generate billions in annual revenues and employ millions of Americans.

- Human Genome Project (1988 to 2010, cost $5.9 billion, an average $450 million annually, in 2012 dollars) is just beginning to yield its benefits. Genomics is like the Internet in the early 1990's. It is an enabling technology with vast untapped potential and a myriad of applications, many which are unknown today. Yet, between 1988 and 2010, HGP's economic

---

[8] Costs of US piloted programs by Claude Lafleur, March 8, 2010 and Bureau of Labor Statistics CPI Inflation Calculator to convert into 2012 dollars.

output/impact was $796 billion[9]. On average, annually, between 1988 and 2010, it created the equivalent of 292,308 high-paying jobs. It yielded $6 billion in state and federal taxes in 2010 alone – paying back the federal investment in one year.

The congruence of new enabling technologies is providing the ability to industrialize healthcare. However, just as we are beginning to move in the right direction, vested interest lobbying and misinformation threaten to kill this opportunity.

---

[9] Economic Impact of the Human Genome Project, Prepared by Battelle Technology Partnership Practice, May 2011.

EDMUND L. VALENTINE

# 5 MISINFORMATION

During my Special Forces Officer's training at the Special Warfare Center at Fort Bragg, North Carolina, one of the many things they taught me was the strategic value of misinformation to achieve an objective. Presentation training taught me to limit the number of points made on any one slide to no more than five, but preferably three – and to use the fewest number of words possible. My marketing courses and experience taught me the value of catchy words and phrases and that perception trumps facts. Never in my wildest dreams did I ever expect to see our great democracy being attacked by these very same principles.

Hundreds of millions of dollars are being spent to obscure the healthcare argument from: 1) how do we as a nation exploit the global healthcare opportunity to revitalize our economy, create high-paying jobs, and raise America's quality of life and standard of living, to 2) repeal "Obamacare".

In order to get elected, politicians have to garner voter support. Investments from special interest groups are misinforming us about the issues. In turn, the only way that our politicians can get elected is to come out with short catchy phrases that resonate with the public in order to get their vote.

Unfortunately, most of us do not really delve into the issues...we vote by what we perceive to be the best candidate based upon the messages we receive. In turn, well-funded misinformation campaigns shift the messages politicians use to get elected.

Perception was not as much a problem before our information and communication centered society. Before, we would be influenced by newspaper articles, a limited number of magazine articles, and a limited amount of radio, some TV, friends and the occasional speech. A lot of what we thought was molded by person-to-person interaction. However, today what we think can be manipulated by multichannel campaigns, e.g., TV adds, newspaper, magazines, Facebook, Twitter, blogs, automated telephone messages, email blasts, etc. As we hear the same message said in different ways via different communication channels, we begin to form a perception that trumps the facts.

As an example, some pundits would have us believe that there are vast differences between the 'Massachusetts' Healthcare Plan' passed by Governor Romney and President Obama's 'Patient Protection And Affordable Care Act' (ACA). However, nothing could be farther from the truth.

Jonathan Gruber, the American economist and professor of economics at the Massachusetts Institute of Technology who helped design both plans, has publically stated that the two laws are "the same fu*#ing bill.".

Both programs create exchanges where private insurers compete. Both require individuals to purchase insurance. And both subsidize those who cannot afford it. It is a relatively new way of extending coverage. Massachusetts was the first place it was adopted, and the Affordable Care Act (ACA) was the second.

To find any differences between the two, you must look to the margins as they only differ in inconsequential ways.

- The Individual Mandate – The Massachusetts plan levies a harsher penalty on people who don't buy insurance: $1,200 versus ACA's $695.

- Subsidies - Both plans subsidize people who can't afford to buy insurance on an exchange. The only difference is that Massachusetts gives more money to fewer people (anyone earning up to 300 percent of the poverty level), while the ACA plan gives less money to more people (anyone earning up to 400 percent of the poverty level).

- Employer Mandate - Both plans require employers to provide insurance, and again the differences are marginal. In Massachusetts companies with 11 or more employees must provide insurance or pay a $295 penalty per employee. Under the ACA, companies with 50 or more employees must offer insurance or pay a $2,000 penalty per employee. The Massachusetts plan affects smaller businesses; ACA levies harsher penalties.

- Young Adults - Both plans let children stay on their parents' plan until they are 26 years old. The only difference is that in Massachusetts children can stay on their parents' plan for two years after they are no longer claimed as a dependent or until they turn 26, whichever comes sooner.

- Limits to Benefits - The ACA forbids insurers from placing limits on the benefits someone can receive over their lifetime or in a given year. The Massachusetts plan doesn't, but most Massachusetts plans don't place limits anyway because it could run afoul of the state's Minimum Creditable Coverage regulations.

- Pre-existing Conditions, Rescission - Both plans require insurers to cover pre-existing conditions and prohibit insurers from rescinding coverage retroactively. However, in Massachusetts an insurer can limit coverage of certain pre-existing conditions to six months, whereas there's no limit under the Affordable Care Act.

- Preventative Care - Insurers in Massachusetts are allowed to charge co-pays for preventative care but the program requires insurers to cover preventative care without a deductible. Preventative care is free under the ACA.

- Contraception – The Massachusetts plan doesn't mention contraception, but only because Massachusetts already had a similar mandate. Under the 2002 law, insurers must cover contraception in the same way they cover other prescription drugs. Unlike the ACA, the Massachusetts law didn't require insurers to provide contraception for free, but it did require them to cover it.

Governor Romney, in his bid for the Presidency, has been portrayed as being against insurance mandates and the ACA. However, in a 2009 op-ed article Governor Romney urged President Obama to follow Massachusetts's lead and adopt the healthcare mandate. He wrote, "Using tax penalties, as we did, or tax credits, as others have proposed, encourages 'free riders' to take responsibility for themselves rather than pass their medical costs on to others". In addition, in 2008 during an ABC News debate, where Charlie Gibson pointed out that Governor Romney had "backed away from mandates on a national basis," Governor Romney replied, "No, no, I like mandates. The mandates work.". There are other examples that makes it clear that Governor Romney's resistance to a federal mandate was just recently brought about by political expediency.

The pressure on Governor Romney is a result of heavy lobbying and a coordinated onslaught/campaign funded for the most part by Healthcare Insurers. A June 26, 2012 Forbes article by Rick Ungar, summarized below, highlights the problem. The title of the article is: "Busted! Health Insurers Secretly Spent Huge To Defeat Health Care Reform While Pretending To Support Obamacare".

It is distressing to note that in 2001, Transparency International's Corruption Perceptions Index ranked the United States as the 16th least corrupt country. By last year, we had fallen to 24th place. The World Bank also reports a weakening of corruption controls in the United States since the late 1990s, so we are falling behind most other developed nations.

The following should be of concern to all of us, to every American, as this is the misinformation that is being utilized to sway policy to benefit a specific industry or individuals at the cost of the American people. This, in my opinion, represents "destructive" greed…much the same as what we saw during the home mortgage debacle we are all suffering through. It is a threat to our very way of life. Capitalism cannot function without trust as "Virtually every commercial transaction has within itself an element of trust.".

'According to the National Journal's Influence Alley, at the very same time the American Health Insurance Plans (AHIP)—the health insurance industry super lobby—was cutting a deal with the White House leading to its stated support of the proposed Affordable Care Act legislation, they were secretly funneling huge amounts of money to the Chamber of Commerce to be spent on advertising designed to convince the public that the legislation should be defeated.' They spent a stunning $102.4 million over just 15 months.

'The AHIP spent the money in secret by utilizing a completely legal process of funneling the cash to the Chamber of Commerce, who spent tens of millions of dollars bankrolling efforts to kill healthcare reform, under the radar while putting the giant expenditure on their books under the simple heading of 'advocacy'.

According to the National Journal, the backchannel spending allowed insurers to publicly stake out a pro-reform position while privately funding the leading anti-reform lobbying group in Washington. The behind-the-scenes transfers were particularly hard to track because the law does not require groups to publicly disclose where they are sending the money or who they are receiving it from.

"According to Neera Tanden, who served as the senior advisor for health reform at the Department of Health and Human Services and was a member of the Obama White House health reform team, it was all about the Medical Loss Ratio (MLR)—the provision of the ACA that not only requires the health insurance companies to spend 80 percent of your premium dollars on actual health care expenditures, but further requires that they refund to their customers any amounts they fail to spend as required by the MLR."

This type of duplicitous behavior is what is destroying the very fabric of our nation. The misconduct of the financial industry no longer surprises most Americans. These actions by the health insurance industry fall within the same realm – it is a clear breach of trust designed to reward a few at the cost of the majority. Imagine how insurers would behave when you find yourself or your loved ones in a costly medical emergency!

I cannot think that this behavior would be acceptable to any American. The health insurance industry example of duplicitous behavior is designed to mislead voters and to change the political debate to increase insurance industry profits. It serves as an example of how big money is corrupting our political system and forcing our leaders to change positions.

Increasingly, politicians cannot be elected unless they have big money and unless they position their messages to garner voter support. Unfortunately, voter support has been bought by millions of dollars spent to change voter sentiment, not based upon facts, but on perceptions that will garner their respective supporters personal and corporate gain. Something that is increasingly coming at the cost of the American public.

There is no question that when you have legislation that is around 2,500 pages, there are things within the bill that have to be questioned and/or fixed. The following is a potential example:

(Sec. 3136) Power-Driven Wheelchairs

Revises Medicare payment levels for power-driven wheelchairs and makes it so that only "complex" and "rehabilitative" wheelchairs can be purchased; all others must be rented.

Why can't "all others" be purchased. Does it serve the Medicare system or was this entered by a lobbyist to increase the revenues of the wheel chair manufacturers?

The question for healthcare that we should all be asking both our Democratic and Republican legislators is "what are you doing or what will you be doing to position the United States to benefit from the skyrocketing global healthcare opportunity?". The answer to this question impacts not only your and my family's healthcare but our economic future, as individuals and as a country. Healthcare is at the heart of fixing our economy.

# 6 MISINFORMATION HAS CAUSED ECONOMIC PARALYSIS

Over the last few months we have heard that we have plenty of money for loans and investment but that it continues to sit on the sidelines because individuals and corporations are unwilling to commit – no matter what the Federal Reserve tries. This is caused by uncertainty about what the rules are or will be. Let me use a sports analogy to explain this.

Let's say that I want you to play baseball. . . in order to be willing to play, you want to know the rules and that we will have an impartial referee. You also want to make sure somebody isn't going to come along and change the rules in the middle of the game.

Well, we have all these people and corporations who have money on the sidelines. We are telling them, come on, invest. They reply, "What are the rules?" and we say, "We'll tell you later". Then they ask what about the referee? We then reply with "we're still struggling to figure out who that's going to be". . . . That's not an environment designed to get people to invest, to get people or corporations to play.

This situation of uncertainty can in great part be attributed to the misinformation campaign that has shifted the political dialog. It has not served the Republican Party, the Democratic Party, and most importantly us, the American people. Our political dialog has to be geared to clearly outline how we as a country and as an economy are going to move forward, what the rules are going to be, and that we are not going to be changing the rules in the future. I fear that if we do not do this, we will continue to undermine our economic recovery.

Now let's discuss what is required to fix healthcare so we may capitalize on the global opportunity. To me, it is clear that the key components to fixing U.S. healthcare are in the Patient Protection and Affordable Care Act…also that what is missing are: 1) enabling the industrialization of healthcare and 2) financial incentives and tax regulation to insure that we retain high technology medical products innovation and manufacturing in the United States. The last two issues are the basis of what we should be hearing our representatives, and those aspiring to become our representatives, discussing.

.

EDMUND L. VALENTINE

# 7 ELECTRONIC MEDICAL RECORDS

Interoperable electronic medical records (EMRs) is an enabling technology. It isn't just about capturing our medical information, it is about enabling better quality, less costly, less duplicative, state of the art, more convenient care while simultaneously increasing patient satisfaction.

Having electronic medical records allows coordinated care. This means that eventually we will routinely be able to go to places like CVS, Walgreens, and WalMart, that have retail clinics, for some routine medical care at a significantly lower cost and increased convenience versus going to our physician's office or the emergency room. Our primary care physicians will, via the interoperable electronic medical record, see the results of any visits to allied health professional, specialists, emergency room, etc. and will be able to monitor/manage our care.

Connectivity enables the concept of the "Medical Home" where our primary care doctors will be responsible and paid for keeping us well.

Electronic medical records also serve as the backbone behind cybernetics supported care. Cybernetics allows the comparison of data with other people that have the same physical profile, blood values, diagnostic readouts, and symptoms. Think of it as the Google of healthcare...however, more powerful. The system continues to refine its accuracy each time it is queried. It was launched in 2012 by IBM and will increasingly be utilized to assist in establishing: 1) a diagnosis, and 2) the most cost-effective and efficacious course of therapy specifically tailored for each of us. It also promises to allow nurse practitioners, allied health professionals, and physician's assistants to increasingly carry out more of the routine roles historically filled by physicians, e.g., enabling less costly physician extenders.

Think of Star Wars, this is our Medical Droid. We need cybernetics because medical knowledge is doubling every two years...and is expected to double in less than one year by 2020. No physician can keep up with the change. As a result of cybernetics, we should be decreasing the average 17 years it takes for the best treatments and practices to become routine care.

Electronic medical records software has little more value than paper medical records if the different software packages are not able to talk with each other. On the surface, this would appear simple, but it is not. The average U.S. hospital has over ≥200 computer systems that have to be integrated. There are over 365 electronic medical records vendors with a myriad of software offerings.

This quagmire required interoperability standards to allow data to be interchanged...and networks to be established to exchange the data on a regional and national basis. Financial incentives were also needed to entice providers to convert their records and systems and processes into user friendly electronic medical data/records.

Both the American Recovery and Reinvestment Act of 2009 and the Patient Protection and Affordable Care Act (ACA) of March 23, 2010 have been instrumental in the roll out and increasing utilization of interoperable electronic medical records. It is not just the technology, but standards and financial incentives that are making this possible. Adoption would not be happening and we as individuals and as a society would not be garnering the benefits, which will be exploding over the foreseeable future, without the legislation.

These technologies, e.g., electronic medical records, systems, integrated care systems, processes, cybernetics, etc. all have potential multi-billion dollar global markets.

# 8 CHANGE
# PROVIDER REIMBURSEMENT

When we buy something we expect what we pay for. When we are paid to do something, we try to do what we are being asked to do in order to get paid.

We have to change how providers, e.g., doctors, hospitals, nursing facilities, etc., are compensated from procedures to outcomes and from fee-for-service to wellness. That is the only way we will get the inefficiencies out of the United States healthcare system.

Cars serve as a good example to illustrate this point. Limited attention was paid to product quality as long as the buyer had to pay for both the parts and labor as they wore out - regardless of how quickly this happened. However, when competitors saw an opportunity to increase share by: 1) first, improving a products quality and average product life, e.g., brake pads, tires, batteries, etc., and, 2) thereafter differentiating their value proposition and highlighting their reliability by providing a warranty stating that the product would last for a defined period of time, all competitors' quality went up, the lifespans of the products increased, and prices decreased due to competition.

If we have a surgery, for example, we should not have to pay to correct an error made by the physician during surgery and/or the required costs to treat a hospital or facility caused complication, e.g., a nosocomial (hospital acquired) infection. That is the same thinking as if you had a new alternator installed in your car that stopped working a few days after installation. The garage would be responsible for both replacement and labor. This gives the garage and the mechanic incentives to insure that the right product is installed properly the first time.

Today, we all know that it is cheaper to conduct preventative service on our cars rather than wait for a major breakdown. Manufacturers go as far as putting warning systems in new cars and certain car parts to alert the driver before service is needed. This enabled car companies to begin differentiating their products by offering free preventative service for a period of time after a new car or certified used car purchase.

For these automobiles, the dealer's focus is on preventative services to keep repair costs down in order to benefit from certain dealer incentives. It has shifted their orientation from repairs to maintenance. The same thing is starting to be done in healthcare.

A shift from a fee-for-service system to compensation based upon patient wellness forces the primary care physician to fundamentally change how they practice medicine. They are compensated on meeting certain wellness measures for the patients under their care. Their interest is in establishing baselines for each patient and towards early intervention to preclude costly episodes of care. In some instances this means a costly procedure now rather than a considerably more costly procedure in the future.

Provider compensation formulas in and of themselves are innovations. There are a number of innovations ongoing to change provider compensation. Some will work and others will not. This means that different models have to be experimented with before an optimal standard of compensation will materialize. However, the underlying

41

theme in all the compensation formulas is to allow providers to share in the savings generated by wellness management in order to avoid more costly interventions and chronic conditions.

A number of models and demonstration programs are being supported by both private insurance and Medicare/Medicaid, e.g., Accountable Care Organizations, the Medical Home, contracting that will not pay for care required to correct medical mistakes, etc. A number of these have funding under the Accountable Care Act as well as by payers. They are all being enabled by new technologies and electronic medical records.

# 9 COMMODITIZE
# HEALTH INSURANCE

Today, health insurance is a disaster. Every day we hear
about another insult by the health insurance industry on a
patient in their hour of need…or a major surprise when they
get a healthcare bill. We also hear that 60 percent of United
States bankruptcies are as a result of healthcare bills…and
that during the first six months of 2011, one in three
Americans lived in a family that had trouble paying its
medical bills within the previous year; was currently paying a
medical bill over time; or currently had a medical bill the
family was unable to pay at all[10].

---

[10] According to a survey of more than 50,000 people by the
National Center for Health Statistics, part of the Centers for
Disease Control and Prevention.

I'd like to share a recent but minor experience to help illustrate the problem with health insurance. Recently a person that I will refer to as Mary changed her health insurance. The new policy included 100% coverage for preventative services including an annual physical. Mary has been getting the same physical for over twenty years. After her most recent physical, which found no changes whatsoever, she got billed for some routine services that should have been covered by her health insurance.

The following illustrates just how broken our health insurance system is, how wasteful it is, and just how under reported the waste is if we took into account the time spent by patients, physicians and provider support staff to correct billing errors.

- When Mary contacted her insurance company about the bills for preventative care, they stated that the doctor had used the wrong code and that the doctor had to submit a new invoice with the changed code.
- She contacted the doctor and they changed the code and submitted a new invoice.
- Then the insurance company informed her that a preventative diagnostic procedure was not covered even

though the diagnostic test had been a routine part of Mary's physical for the prior twenty years and one her doctor wanted continued.

- When she asked what was included in preventative care, the insurance company representative was not sure. After about thirty minutes she came back and said that the list was on their website. When Mary went to the website, the list was not clear.

- During this review, she found out that she had been paying out-of-pocket for a routine annual eye exam. The insurance company representative stated that she needed to contact the health system that provided her care to get reimbursed.

- When she called the health system, Mary was informed that she needed the doctor to change the code before they would rebate any money (keep in mind that the doctor was part of the health system) as he coded the visit as a diagnostic visit rather than the annual eye exam visit which Mary had specifically scheduled (I know you will be surprised to learn that a diagnostic visit has a higher reimbursement versus the same visit listed as a routine eye exam). Mary and her husband were then informed that the health system probably would not provide reimbursement as this was not a routine eye exam as a diagnosis had been made- which Mary and her husband were unaware of.

- When they asked what the diagnosis was, they were told that it could not be supplied due to patient confidentiality requirements under HIPPA regulations. In turn, Mary's husband informed the representative, with Mary also on the phone, that by law she was entitled to see the record. The representative then said he would forward a request/authority form right away…it never arrived.

- At this point Mary and her husband had over four hours of time each for a $150.00 charge…the system also had at least that much time into this effort….and they were not close to being able to get reimbursed…I am sending a copy of this book to the head of the University of Miami Health System to give him another insight of how patient centered his accounting group is.

Imagine what would happen if this had been a major medical event!

When we buy health insurance we should know what we are buying and should not be surprised with a bill after we receive care. We should also be able to compare policies and then make our decisions based upon coverage, price and the quality reputation of the insurance company.

It is ludicrous to expect that someone that goes into an "in-network hospital" for a covered procedure provided by an "in-network" doctor will get a post-surgery bill for an "out-of-network" anesthesiologist that was chosen by the "in-network" hospital.

Today under Medicare, if we want to buy a Medicare supplement plan (given you are old enough for Medicare), the alternatives are standardized from Plan A to Plan J. What is covered is clearly spelled out and competition is strictly on price and the reputation of the insurance company. When you talk to an agent, they say buy my supplemental coverage and I will help you figure out which drug plan would be best for you. The insurance has been made into a predicable commodity which offers the exact same coverage regardless of which insurance company offers the plan. The only difference is price.

As to the Medicare drug plans, they are all over the place....and if someone picks the wrong plan, they can be paying hundreds of dollars more per month versus another drug insurance plan for the same medication...a very educated friend of mine that had been a high level executive in a very large company just got caught with the wrong plan for medications he had been taking for years.

The Affordable Care Act contains 26 coordinated insurance reform implementation steps, that began taking place in 2010, that will be implemented through 2018 to move health insurance toward a commodity product:

### 2010
1. Review of Health Plan Premium Increases
2. Pre-existing Condition Insurance Plan
3. Consumer Website
4. Adult Dependent Coverage To Age 26
5. Consumer Protection In Insurance
6. Insurance Plan Appeals Process
7. Coverage of Preventative Benefits

### 2011
8. Minimum Medical Loss Ratio for Insurers
9. Funding for Health Insurance Exchanges

### 2012
10. State Notification Regarding Exchanges
11. CO-OP Health Insurance Plans

### 2014
12. Individual Requirement to Have Insurance
13. Free Choice Vouchers
14. Health Insurance Exchanges
15. Health Insurance Premium and Cost Sharing Subsidies
16. Guaranteed Availability of Insurance
17. No Annual Limits on Coverage
18. Essential Health Benefits
19. Multi-State Health Plans

20. Temporary Reimbursement Program for Health Plans
21. Basic Health Plan
22. Employer Requirements
23. Wellness Programs in Insurance
24. Fees on Health Insurance Sector
**2016**
25. Health Care Choice Compacts
**2018**
26. Tax on High-Cost Insurance

We should all keep in mind that absent of any outside intervention, such as patents or some kind of regulatory protection, all products and industries eventually become commodities. Ironically, health insurance started as a commodity. It became a differentiated product offering when insurance companies began to realize that they could increase their margins/profitability while offering competitive prices to their customers by underwriting, i.e., not covering more costly individuals. Protection from commoditization was also offered by states precluding cross-state line competition. Further differentiation was provided by the level of coverage offered versus the premium charged.

Today it is very difficult for most of us to know what we are buying, what we are paying for, and what we are entitled to when we buy health insurance. The provisions in the Accountable Care Plan are trying to use the government's role as the biggest healthcare payer and certain marketplace legislation to enable the move of health insurance back into a commodity product. In turn, marketplace competition can be utilized to drive costs out of the system.

# 10 INDUSTRIALIZE HEALTHCARE

We cannot regulate and/or legislate to fix healthcare; it is too large and too complex. Our annual $2.8 trillion healthcare expenditures would qualify as the six largest country, by gross domestic product (GDP), in the world. Larger than Russia, the sixth largest economy, and slightly less than Germany, the fifth largest economy. Our ~17 million healthcare employees would qualify as the fifth largest state, by population, after Florida...and significantly larger than the population of the fifth largest state, Illinois. In addition, our healthcare industry is comprised of over 125,000 companies and organizations spread throughout our 50 states.

The only way we can fix U.S. healthcare is by enabling free market competition. Free marketplace competition has to be able to take place on a local, regional and national basis. To enable competition we will have to rescind or modify different regulations or legislation at the federal, state, county and city levels that precludes competition, e.g., certificates of need (CONs), Federal Trade Commission blockage of provider mergers or acquisition, and regulations that preclude across state line competition serve as examples.

Enabling free market competition to correct the inefficiencies in our system are not addressed in current healthcare legislation (Accountable Care Act, etc.). This is an issue that needs to be addressed by our federal, state, county and city legislators.

# 11 FINANCIAL INCENTIVES AND TAX REGULATION

We are beginning to lose high-technology high-paying healthcare product innovation and manufacturing jobs to other countries. Yet, we do not appear to be looking at pharmaceuticals, medical devices, in vitro diagnostics, medical equipment, medical supplies, etc. as global opportunities.

Healthcare is one of the few skyrocketing global opportunities that is required by virtually every man, woman or child in the world…and one which can be an economic engine for us. A question that needs to be asked and addressed by our representatives in Washington is "What do we have to do to retain high-technology healthcare products innovation and manufacturing in the United States…what are the financial incentives, investments, and tax policies that will make us competitive on a world market basis.

Our middle class, our standard of living, and our future economic growth will be impacted by the investments the government will make in supporting research, development, education, immigration, and high technology job creation. If we fix healthcare, we will go a long way to fixing the economy. If we fail, we will destroy our middle class and our standard of living. Our debates on government's role in the United States should center on healthcare and how we will be capitalizing on this opportunity.

We need incentives and support for the development of base technologies, new products and services, and new companies. We also need incentives to keep and revitalize our high technology medical industries.

Tax regulation must be amended to reward companies for investing in the creation and growth of high technology medical products and job and company creations. The focus must be on government partnering with our respective industries to provide a business friendly environment that encourages serving global healthcare markets.

The question for our representatives is what specifically have you done, what specifically are you doing, and what specifically do you plan to do to insure we retain and maintain or increase our global healthcare products innovation and manufacturing leadership?

EDMUND L. VALENTINE

# 12 EDUCATION AND IMMIGRATION

Advances in life sciences, including pharmaceuticals, biotechnology, medical devices, in vitro diagnostics, medical equipment and medical supplies, were a major driver of global economic growth in the second half of the twentieth century. Since World War II, we, the United States, have stood firmly at the forefront of the life sciences revolution. Our leadership was built upon a solid commitment to robust and sustained federal investment in biomedical research and development (R&D).

Federal investments laid the foundation for the development of scores of breakthrough drugs, therapies, and medical devices - from personalized gene therapies, synthetic skin, imaging systems, the artificial pancreas, etc. to cures for certain types of cancer. Federal investments in R&D

57

catalyzed the development of our globally competitive, high-wage life sciences industry (as well as our other high technology industries). Today, our life sciences industry supports more than seven million jobs and annually contributes $69 billion, almost five percent, of our gross domestic product (GDP). But our leadership of the global life sciences industry is under threat.

A growing number of countries, including China, Germany, India, Singapore, Sweden, the United Kingdom, and others have recognized that life sciences represents a high-wage, high-growth industry opportunity. They have significantly expanded their financial support for biomedical research, they have implemented a range of policies designed to enhance their biomedical innovation ecosystems, they have and are passing tax incentives that apply a lower tax rate to income derived from patented product revenues (to attract high-technology industries to innovate, develop, and manufacture high technology products in their country), they have instituted regulatory reforms to speed approvals, and immigration and education policies have been designed to attract and to educate the best life sciences talent. They are making these investments to take the leadership in these industries away from us, from the United States.

They have studied what has worked in creating economic growth, they have found strong evidence that our growth engine is the American research university model. Our model is a unique blend of the best and brightest students from around the world, top quality professors with aggressive research programs, and a close association with private industry and venture financing. This model has combined to spin off entrepreneurs with bright ideas for the next generation products, services, and new companies.

Stanford University and the University of California at Berkeley were the catalysts for Silicon Valley, and the Massachusetts Institute of Technology has been the parent of thousands of start-up companies along Route 128 in Massachusetts. Other countries have their prestigious universities; however, none matches ours when it comes down to spinning off smart people with smart ideas and the resultant wealth creation. However, other countries are now investing to duplicate our university model.

China serves as an excellent example. It has designated biotechnology as one of seven key strategic and emerging (SEI) pillar industries and has pledged to invest $308.5 billion in biotechnology over the next five years. This means that, if current trends in biomedical research investment continue, our government's investment in life sciences research over the ensuing half-decade is likely to be barely half that of China's in current dollars, and roughly one-quarter of China's level as a share of GDP.

Most Americans will be shocked to learn that in the first half of 2010, BGI, a privately-operated Chinese institute, had more gene sequencing capacity than the entire United States and about one-third of total global capacity. To fulfill its mission, the institute assembled an army of young bioinformaticians. They are gearing up to mass-produce cheap, quality genome sequences. This, in turn, may accelerate development of cost-effective, DNA-related diagnostic tests, clinical laboratory assays, and products for patient care.

We are being challenged at the very time where our politics has come into play to weaken a deteriorating situation. Other countries are investing relatively more in biomedical R&D as a share of their economies. Our funding for biomedical research peaked in 2003, in both inflation-adjusted dollars and as a share of GDP, and has been slipping since. Our tax policies for our life science companies are becoming increasingly less attractive at the same time that competing countries are making theirs more attractive. Our immigration policies and decreasing federal research funding have resulted in foreign students, that we have educated and that we need to reinvigorate our economy, going back to their home countries.

The brain-drain trend threatens our dominance as the research and innovation center of the world. It is jeopardizing our businesses that are seeking to innovate, develop, manufacture, and sell cutting-edge products. In addition, less innovation in universities means fewer startups and less commercialization of products. If a scientist is not available in the United States, companies will invest overseas – and for each scientist, we will lose an additional three to five support jobs that would have been created.

Another problem we have is the lack of consistency and predictability in the level of government biomedical research funding. As discussed earlier, uncertainty leads to investment paralysis.

The 2009 American Recovery and Reinvestment Act (ARRA) included a welcome, but temporary, increase in National Institutes of Health (NIH) funding. But the short lived positive increase has not been maintained. NIH funding is threatened with a drastic rollback by the looming automatic sequestration scheduled to be triggered January 2, 2013 (unless Congress reaches a budget deal in the interim). The sequestration would slash NIH funding by at least 7.8 percent, leading to a $2.4 billion reduction in 2013, the largest cut in the agency's history.

Funding uncertainty makes it difficult for researchers, research institutions, and businesses to make long-term planning and investment decisions in an industry where base technology research and product development spans a period of years. In such an environment of constrained and uncertain funding levels, private investigators with promising research proposals will increasingly look to pursue opportunities abroad. Our challenge is to have government policies that minimize or eliminate uncertainty in order to sustain robust levels of research, innovation, and product development funding that spins off companies that will revitalize our high technology, high-paying medical products industries, create jobs, raise our standard of living, and put us on a more sustainable economic path.

# 13 THE RIGHT QUESTIONS

The questions that we should be asking our representatives before voting for them is:

"What are you doing or what will you be doing to position the United States to benefit from the skyrocketing global healthcare opportunity?".

"What are you doing or what will you be doing to insure that we retain high paying, high technology medical products innovation and manufacturing in the United States?"

"What are you doing or what will you be doing to reverse America's uncertainty which has sidelined investors and resulted in investment paralysis?"

"What are you doing or what will you be doing to insure that the United States continues to dominate as the research and innovation center of the world?.

"What are you doing or what will you be doing to insure we stay on the forefront of the life sciences revolution?"

If we force our representatives to answer these questions, we will be migrating the discussion to the four substantive issues, healthcare, education, taxation, and immigration, that have to be addressed if the United States is to remain a global economic power.

# ABOUT THE AUTHOR

Edmund L. Valentine is a healthcare industry expert with over 27 years of global healthcare industry experience. He is the author of award winning "Multi-Trillion Dollar U.S. HEALTHCARE TO 2020 Gold Rush", multiple editions of MMC International's "Trends Shaping U.S. Pharmaceutical Industry Strategies" report, which is in its 13th edition, "Trends Shaping U.S. Medical Device Industry Strategies" and is the editor of "Rx Marketer's Reference Guide", 2nd Edition as well as therapeutic area reviews and various articles and Insights pieces. Valentine is Chairman and C.E.O. of MMC International, a strategy, general management, business development, marketing, manufacturing, and technology assessment advisory firm primarily focusing on the global healthcare industry. He is a recognized authority on the trends shaping healthcare.

EDMUND L. VALENTINE

# BOOKS BY
# EDMUND L. VALENTINE

## Consumer Book

*Multi-Trillion Dollar*
*U.S. HEALTHCARE TO 2020*
*Gold Rush*
www.healthcaregoldrush.com

The 2012 through 2020 period presents investors and companies with unprecedented opportunities to create wealth. Multi-Trillion Dollar U.S. HEALTHCARE TO 2020 Gold Rush provides insights into the change drivers, enabling technologies, innovations, and industry trends and where and how wealth will be created.

## Trade References

*Trends Shaping U.S. Pharmaceutical Industry Strategies, 13th Edition*
www.rxtrendsreport.com

Rx Marketer's Reference Guide, 2nd Edition
www.rxmarketersreferenceguide.com

*Trends Shaping U.S. Medical Devices Industry Strategies (Medical Devices, In Vitro Diagnostics, Medical Equipment, and Medical Supplies)*
http://www.mmcint.com/books/medicaldevicestrends.html

*2013 U.S. Rx Company Planning Overview*
http://www.mmcint.com/books/2013usrxplanning.html

# EDMUND L. VALENTINE

# KEYNOTE, INFORMATIONAL, AND MOTIVATIONAL SPEECHES

Fix Healthcare, Fix The Economy - Ignore Healthcare, Destroy The Middle Class

The Industrialization of Healthcare

Profit From The U.S. Healthcare Gold Rush

Healthcare Is An Economic Driver

**Contact:**

Media@mmcint.com
MMC International Publications
203-961-9100